THE KANSAS CITY ROYALS

BY
MARK STEWART

NORWOOD HOUSE PRESS
CHICAGO, ILLINOIS

Norwood House Press
P.O. Box 316598
Chicago, Illinois 60631

For information regarding Norwood House Press, please visit our website at:
www.norwoodhousepress.com or call 866-565-2900.

All photos courtesy of Getty Images except the following:
Topps, Inc. (6, 20, 21, 22, 34 top & bottom left, 35 top right, 37, 40, 42 top & bottom left, 43 top),
Black Book Partners Archives (9, 23, 35 bottom, 36, 38, 39, 45), Tom DiPace (11, 14),
Kansas City Royals (33 inset), TCMA Ltd. (34 bottom right), SSPC (41),
Author's Collection (43 bottom left), Fun Foods, Inc. (43 bottom right), Matt Richman (48).
Cover Photo: Jamie Squire/Getty Images

The memorabilia and artifacts pictured in this book are presented for educational and informational purposes,
and come from the collection of the author.

Editor: Mike Kennedy
Designer: Ron Jaffe
Project Management: Black Book Partners, LLC.
Special thanks to Topps, Inc.

Library of Congress Cataloging-in-Publication Data

Stewart, Mark, 1960-
  The Kansas City Royals / by Mark Stewart.
    p. cm. -- (Team spirit)
  Includes bibliographical references and index.
  Summary: "A Team Spirit Baseball edition featuring the Kansas City Royals
that chronicles the history and accomplishments of the team. Includes access
to the Team Spirit website, which provides additional information, updates
and photos"--Provided by publisher.
  ISBN 978-1-59953-484-8 (library : alk. paper) -- ISBN 978-1-60357-364-1
(ebook) 1. Kansas City Royals (Baseball team)--History--Juvenile
literature. I. Title.
  GV875.K3S737 2012
  796.357'6409778411--dc23
                                        2011048465

Manufactured in the United States of America in North Mankato, Minnesota.
196N—012012

COVER PHOTO: The Royals can't wait to celebrate a 2011 victory.

TABLE OF CONTENTS

ABOUT OUR GLOSSARY

In this book, there may be several words that you are reading for the first time. Some are sports words, some are new vocabulary words, and some are familiar words that are used in an unusual way. All of these words are defined on page 46. Throughout the book, sports words appear in **bold type**. Regular vocabulary words appear in ***bold italic type***.

MEET THE ROYALS

When people hear the words "true blue," it makes them think of being loyal. When baseball fans in Kansas and Missouri hear those words, they think of the Kansas City Royals. For the fans and players, true blue means playing hard and playing smart until the final out.

The Royals are always on the lookout for players with a winning attitude. Rather than filling the roster with superstars, Kansas City searches for super people. Even in the years when the team struggles, fans always have something to cheer about.

This book tells the story of the Royals. They teach their players to put the team first. They find ways to win that other teams don't think of. That is why, when things look their very worst, the Royals are often at their very best.

Alex Gordon returns to the dugout after a home run. Young stars like Gordon have kept Royals fans "true blue" for more than 40 years.

GLORY DAYS

Baseball in Kansas City, Missouri has changed quite a bit over the years. Back in the 1880s, real cowboys rode into town to watch a **National League (NL)** team called the Cowboys. In the early 1900s, fans in the city rooted for teams in the **minor leagues** and the **Negro Leagues**. From 1955 to 1967, Kansas City was the hometown of the A's. They now play in Oakland.

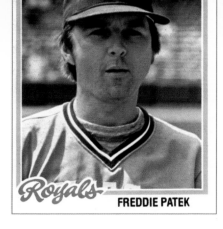

FREDDIE PATEK

The story of the Royals began in 1969. That year, they were one of two new teams in the **American League (AL)**. The Royals won 69 games their first year and put some good players on the field, including Lou Piniella, Pat Kelly, and Bob Oliver.

Over the next few seasons, the Royals made smart trades for Amos Otis, Freddie Patek, Hal McRae, and John Mayberry. They also developed several good players on their own, including Paul Splittorff, Steve Busby, Frank White, and George Brett. After a

coach named Charlie Lau taught the Royals a new way of hitting, their batting averages soared. By 1976, Kansas City had one of the best teams in baseball.

The Royals reminded many people of old-time clubs. The players were tough and were always thinking of new ways to win games. They could beat you with their bats, their gloves, their arms, or their feet. If an opponent lost focus for even an inning, the Royals were likely to win the game.

From 1973 to 1985, Kansas City finished first or second in the **AL West** 12 times. The Royal advanced to the **American League Championship Series (ALCS)** three years in a row from 1976 to 1978. Each time, they lost to the New York Yankees. They finally beat the "Bronx Bombers" in 1980 to win their first **pennant**. Joining Brett, White, and McRae on that team were relief pitcher Dan Quisenberry and speedy outfielder Willie Wilson.

Kansas City's first championship came in 1985. That team featured the same hitting stars, but a new group of starters led the pitching staff. Bret Saberhagen, Mark Gubicza, Danny Jackson, and Charlie Leibrandt gave the Royals the boost they needed to defeat the St. Louis Cardinals in a thrilling **World Series**.

As new players replaced old ones in the Kansas City lineup, victories were harder and harder to come by. The Royals had only three winning seasons during the 1990s. At the same time, some fans stopped coming to the park. With ticket sales down, Kansas City did not have as much money to spend as many other teams did. It became more difficult for the Royals to compete. The team

LEFT: George Brett   **ABOVE**: Bret Saberhagen

responded by developing young players such as Kevin Appier, Brian McRae, Johnny Damon, and Mike Sweeney.

The most devoted Kansas City fans never stopped rooting for their team during those long seasons. They also came to appreciate just how good the clubs of the 1970s and 1980s were. As the 21st century began, they kept coming to the ballpark to see the new stars who wore the Royals uniform. Those players included Carlos Beltran, Raul Ibanez, David DeJesus, John Buck, Zack Greinke, Luke Hochevar, Joakim Soria, Alej26x Gordon, Billy Butler, Mike Moustakas, and Eric Hosmer.

Not all of these players stayed in a Royals uniform. Sometimes, to build a winner, a team has to trade its stars of today in order to improve for tomorrow. Kansas City fans were sad to see favorites like Damon, Beltran, and Greinke go to other cities. However, their hope is that the players the team trades for will become stars—and that soon they will form the heart of a championship club.

LEFT: Mike Sweeney and Johnny Damon celebrate a home run.
ABOVE: Zack Greinke

HOME TURF

For their first four seasons, the Royals played in Municipal Stadium. In 1973, the team moved to brand-new Royals Stadium. It was built right next to Arrowhead Stadium, the home of the Kansas City Chiefs football team.

In 1993, the Royals renamed their stadium in honor of their original owner, Ewing Kauffman. The team also began making improvements to the ballpark. In 1995, the Royals switched from *artificial turf* to grass. Later, the team installed a huge high-definition scoreboard. The Royals also added statues around the stadium of George Brett, Frank White, and Kauffman and his wife, Muriel. Another feature that fans love is the fountain located behind the outfield fence. It is 322 feet wide and has waterfalls that are 10 feet high.

BY THE NUMBERS

- The Royals' stadium has 37,903 seats.
- The distance from home plate to the left field foul pole is 330 feet.
- The distance from home plate to the center field fence is 410 feet.
- The distance from home plate to the right field foul pole is 330 feet.

Kauffman Stadium rises behind a statue of Ewing Kauffman and his wife, Muriel.

DRESSED FOR SUCCESS

Royal blue has been the team's main team color since its first season. In 1973, the Royals changed their road uniforms from gray to powder blue. This shade of blue was used by several teams during the 1970s. The Royals featured it until the early 1990s, when they switched back to gray road uniforms. The team also used a sleeveless style for a few seasons. Today, for special occasions, the Royals choose between two jerseys. One is royal blue, and the other is light blue.

The team's cap has remained the same since 1969. It is blue with the hometown initials, *KC*, in white. The Royals also wear a patch on their left sleeve with the team *logo*. It includes a small yellow crown. Across the front of their uniforms, the team writes its name in script, with *Royals* at home and *Kansas City* on the road.

LEFT: Eric Hosmer wears one of the team's 2011 uniforms.
ABOVE: John Mayberry poses in Kansas City's 1973 road uniform.

WE WON!

Unlike some new teams, the Royals developed into a championship *contender* within a few years of their first season. Their fans supported them every step of the way. They believed the club would reach the World Series and win a championship in the 1970s. The Royals came close. Three years

in a row—in 1976, 1977, and 1978—they faced the New York Yankees in the ALCS. Each time, Kansas City suffered heartbreaking losses.

The Royals finally won their first pennant in 1980. Many of their stars from the '70s were still on the team, including George Brett, Frank White, Hal McRae, Dennis Leonard, and Paul Splittorff. When the Royals lost in the World Series that fall, there was great sadness in Kansas City. It seemed as if the team had missed its big chance.

LEFT: George Brett and the Royals were given a parade after the 1980 season.　**RIGHT**: Frank White completes a double play during the 1985 World Series.

Five seasons later, the Royals made it back to the World Series. The 1985 team was led by a group of talented pitchers, including Bret Saberhagen, Danny Jackson, Mark Gubicza, Bud Black, Charlie Leibrandt, and Dan Quisenberry. The Royals beat the Toronto Blue Jays in a thrilling ALCS. Brett topped all Kansas City hitters in the series with a .348 average.

The Royals played the St. Louis Cardinals in the World Series. Fans called it the "I-70" series for the name of the highway that connects the two cities. The Royals and Cardinals were evenly matched. People in Missouri could hardly wait for the teams to take the field. When the Cardinals won the first two games in Kansas City, it looked like St. Louis might capture the championship without breaking a sweat. But the Royals fought back.

In Game 3 in St. Louis, Saberhagen showed why he was the AL's **Cy Young Award** winner. He struck out eight batters and gave up

only six hits in Kansas City's 6–1 victory. Unfortunately, the Cardinals responded with a win in Game 4 to take a big lead in the series.

Kansas City manager Dick Howser told his players to relax and focus on one game at a time. Jackson was brilliant on the mound in Game 5, and the Royals won 5–1. Game 6 was tense from the opening pitch. Kansas City trailed 1–0 going into the bottom of the ninth inning.

Jorge Orta led off for the Royals and hit a grounder to Jack Clark. The St. Louis first baseman caught the ball and flipped it to pitcher Todd Worrell, who was covering first. The throw beat Orta to the base, but the umpire called him safe. Suddenly, the Royals and their fans had new life.

Next, Steve Balboni hit a foul pop that no one caught. Given a second chance, the Kansas City slugger stroked a single. When a pitch got away from the catcher, the runners moved up to second and third. The Cardinals walked McRae in order to face pinch-hitter Dane Iorg instead. Iorg hit a single that brought home the winning runs!

The Royals and their fans were brimming with confidence heading into Game 7, especially with Saberhagen ready to take the ball. He was spectacular again. The Royals scored five runs early

in the game, and then added six more for an 11–0 victory. Kansas City became the first team ever to lose the first two games of a World Series at home and then come back to take the championship.

Brett and Willie Wilson led the hitting attack, but Saberhagen was the difference for the Royals. He pitched two great games—the second coming one day after the birth of his son. Saberhagen was named **Most Valuable Player (MVP)** of the series.

LEFT: Dane Iorg gets a handshake after his winning hit.
ABOVE: The Royals celebrate after their victory in Game 7.

GO-TO GUYS

To be a true star in baseball, you need more than a quick bat and a strong arm. You have to be a "go-to guy"—someone the manager wants on the pitcher's mound or in the batter's box when it matters most. Fans of the Royals have had a lot to cheer about over the years, including these great stars …

THE PIONEERS

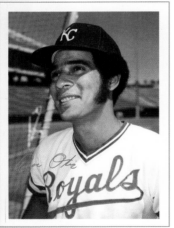

AMOS OTIS   Outfielder

• BORN: 4/26/1947   • PLAYED FOR TEAM: 1970 TO 1983

Amos Otis was the Royals' first big star. He was a good hitter, a great fielder, and a swift baserunner. Many of Kansas City's opponents thought Otis was the team's most important player during the 1970s.

PAUL SPLITTORFF   Pitcher

• BORN: 10/8/1946   • DIED: 5/25/2011
• PLAYED FOR TEAM: 1970 TO 1984

The Royals **drafted** Paul Splittorff in 1968. He spent his entire career with Kansas City and was one of their best pitchers. In 1973, Splittorff became the first Royal to win 20 games in a season.

HAL McRAE   Designated Hitter

- BORN: 7/10/1945   • PLAYED FOR TEAM: 1973 TO 1987

Hal McRae gave the Royals toughness and a winning attitude when they needed it most. With his hard hitting and daring baserunning, he helped the team become a winner.

FRANK WHITE   Second Baseman

- BORN: 9/4/1950   • PLAYED FOR TEAM: 1973 TO 1990

Frank White did whatever the team needed— and did it very well. He won eight **Gold Gloves** and was an **All-Star** five times. White spent his entire career with the Royals.

GEORGE BRETT   Third Baseman

- BORN: 5/15/1953   • PLAYED FOR TEAM: 1973 TO 1993

George Brett's smooth, short swing produced screaming line drives and sizzling grounders. Brett batted .390 in 1980 and was one of the game's best fielders year in and year out.

FRANK WHITE

DENNIS LEONARD   Pitcher

- BORN: 5/8/1951   • PLAYED FOR TEAM: 1974 TO 1986

Dennis Leonard wasn't afraid of any hitter. He dared them to swing at his best pitches and usually came out on top. He was a 20-game winner three times from 1977 to 1980.

LEFT: Amos Otis   **ABOVE**: Frank White

WILLIE WILSON   Outfielder

- BORN: 7/9/1955
- PLAYED FOR TEAM: 1976 TO 1990

Willie Wilson had the speed and size to be a football star, but he chose baseball instead. He had 230 hits in 1980 and led the AL with a .332 average in 1982. Wilson stole more than 600 bases with the Royals.

DAN QUISENBERRY   Pitcher

- BORN: 2/7/1953   • DIED: 9/30/1998
- PLAYED FOR TEAM: 1979 TO 1988

Dan Quisenberry did not throw hard, but his unusual sidearm style kept hitters from taking their best swings. That was all he needed to become the league's best relief pitcher in the early 1980s.

BRET SABERHAGEN   Pitcher

- BORN: 4/11/1964   • PLAYED FOR TEAM: 1984 TO 1991

Three years after pitching in high school, Bret Saberhagen was blowing away the St. Louis Cardinals in Game 7 of the 1985 World Series. He was Kansas City's most electrifying player during the 1980s.

ABOVE: Willie Wilson   **RIGHT**: Alex Gordon

BO JACKSON   Outfielder

- BORN: 11/30/1962   • PLAYED FOR TEAM: 1986 TO 1990

Bo Jackson was already a famous football player when he joined the Royals in 1986. His amazing talent shone through again and again. Fans did not miss an inning when Jackson played—at any time he might do something they had never seen before!

ALEX GORDON   Outfielder

- BORN: 2/10/1984
- FIRST YEAR WITH TEAM: 2007

Alex Gordon struggled at third base when he first came to the Royals. The team asked him to play left field instead. In 2011, Gordon batted over .300 and won a Gold Glove.

ERIC HOSMER   First Baseman

- BORN: 10/24/1989
- FIRST YEAR WITH TEAM: 2011

Eric Hosmer had been a great power hitter in the minors. Kansas City fans could hardly wait for him to join the Royals. As a **rookie**, Hosmer batted .293 and hit 19 home runs.

CALLING THE SHOTS

The Royals have always counted on their managers to get the best out of their players. The team has also looked for leaders who know how to outsmart their opponents. Almost from the beginning, the Royals have found managers who have been good at both. Kansas City was one of four clubs that began in 1969. Of that group, the Royals were by far the best in the 1970s and 1980s.

Bob Lemon managed the team to its first winning season, in 1971. Lemon had been an All-Star during the 1950s. He taught Kansas City's young pitchers how to fool batters into swinging at balls they could only pop in the air or hammer into the ground. Jack McKeon also led the team in the early 1970s. He was one of the smartest people in baseball.

From 1975 to 1986, the Royals had three good managers: Whitey Herzog, Jim Frey, and Dick Howser. Kansas City went to the **playoffs** seven times during those 12 seasons. George Brett was the star of those teams. The Royals did a good job building their roster around him. Kansas City didn't have a bunch of superstars. But once

Team founder Ewing Kauffman poses with Bo Jackson, one of the club's brightest stars during the 1980s.

the Royals hit the field, it was a different story. No team ever looked forward to a series in Kansas City.

The man who hired all those managers was the team's owner, Ewing Kauffman. He had a good mind for business and a big heart for the people who worked for him. Kauffman never stopped experimenting with ways to make the Royals better. He was just as eager to show the fans in his hometown a good time at the ballpark. Kauffman ran the Royals for almost 25 years before he passed away at the age of 76 in 1993.

ONE GREAT DAY

George Brett hit many unforgettable home runs for the Royals. None was more important than the one he slammed against the New York Yankees in the 1980 ALCS. In years past, the Royals had come within a few hits or a few pitches of winning the pennant. Somehow, the Yankees always found a way to beat them.

As the series began in 1980, the fans in Kansas City were nervous. Even after the Royals won the first two games, people in Missouri prepared for the worst. Millions watched Game 3 on television. When New York scored twice in the sixth inning, the fans in Yankee Stadium roared with delight. They had a feeling their team would defeat the Royals once again.

With two outs in the seventh inning, Willie Wilson hit a double to right field. The Yankees called for their best relief pitcher, Goose Gossage. He was the meanest, hardest-throwing reliever in baseball. Gossage challenged U L Washington with a sizzling fastball. He fought it off and reached first base safely with a single.

George Brett watches a ball soar toward the upper deck in Yankee Stadium.

Up came Brett. He had finished the season with an amazing .390 average. It was power against power. Gossage fired a fastball, and Brett met it with his short, smooth swing. The ball soared into the upper deck for a three-run homer and a 4–2 lead.

The Yankees loaded the bases in the eighth inning with no outs. Dan Quisenberry "put out the fire," and the Royals went on to win the game and the pennant. It was the day that Kansas City fans had been dreaming of since 1969.

LEGEND HAS IT

WHO WAS THE TEAM'S BEST UNWANTED PLAYER?

LEGEND HAS IT that Lou Piniella was. A lot of teams had gone sour on "Sweet Lou" during his baseball career. From 1962 to 1968, he belonged to the Cleveland Indians, Washington Senators, Baltimore Orioles, and then the Indians again. He was picked in a special draft by the Seattle Pilots in 1969, but the club traded him away before the season started. Piniella became a Royal in time to play on Opening Day. The player no one wanted ended up being Kansas City's top hitter in 1969 and was named the **Rookie of the Year**.

ABOVE: The Royals were Lou Piniella's fifth team.

WHO MADE THE GREATEST DEFENSIVE PLAY IN ROYALS HISTORY?

LEGEND HAS IT that Bo Jackson did—though fans argue which of his gems was the best. In a 1989 game, Jackson fielded a hit off the wall and fired a strike to home plate, 350 feet away. The runner starting on second base was shocked when he found the catcher waiting for him with the baseball! A year later, Jackson caught a long drive near the outfield wall. Instead of crashing into it, he ran up the fence *parallel* to the ground before coming back down.

WHICH PLAYER MADE THE ROYALS SWEAT THE MOST?

LEGEND HAS IT that Mike Moustakas did. The Royals had the second pick in the 2007 draft. They took Moustakas, a high school shortstop who had set home run records in California. Moustakas could either sign a contract with the Royals or enroll in college. The rules said he had to make up his mind by midnight on August 15. Moustakas waited until 11:49 that night before he agreed to play for the Royals. He signed a contract with just 11 minutes to spare!

Whenever the Royals needed a big hit against the New York Yankees, George Brett seemed to be in the batter's box. Brett especially loved to swing the bat at Yankee Stadium. New York's pitchers could never figure out how to get him out, and the park's right field fence was an easy target.

By the summer of 1983, the Yankees and their fans were tired of watching Brett beat them. In a game that July in New York, the Royals trailed 4–3 in the top of the ninth inning. Brett stepped to the plate with a runner on base. Goose Gossage tried to blow a fastball by him, but Brett crushed the pitch into the right field seats for a two-run home run.

After Brett circled the bases, New York manager Billy Martin emerged from his dugout and asked to see the Kansas City star's bat. Martin convinced umpire Tim McClelland to measure the amount of **pine tar** on it. When McClelland ruled the bat had too much of the sticky substance, he called Brett out.

Brett charged out of his dugout to argue. He couldn't decide who he was more angry at, Martin or McClelland. Kansas City manager

George Brett kisses the bat that got him into a sticky situation.

Dick Howser also argued loudly. The Royals decided to protest the game. To their great delight, McClelland's call was overruled. That meant Brett's home run counted, and the game had to be completed.

Nearly four weeks later, the Royals returned to Yankee Stadium and put the finishing touches on a 5–4 victory. Fans would forever call the contest the "Pine Tar Game," and Brett continued to haunt the Yankees for another 10 years.

TEAM SPIRIT

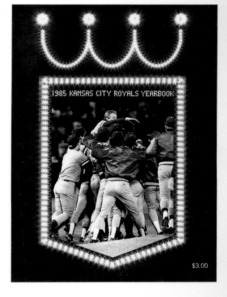

$3.00

W hen the A's left Kansas City for Oakland after the 1967 season, the city was promised that it would get a new team by 1971. As it turned out, fans had to go without baseball for only one season. They were thrilled to hear that their new team would begin play in 1969. With little time to pick a team name, the owners left it up to the fans. They voted for "Royals." This name comes from Kansas City's famous livestock, horse, and rodeo show, which is now called the American Royal.

The Royals have always made a point of keeping the people of Kansas City involved in the team. Often a fan sings the national anthem before games. There are fun play areas for children all over the stadium. The team's mascot, Sluggerrr, is never far away. What is the most popular part of the ballpark? That might just be the barbecue counter. Barbecue is Kansas City's most famous food.

LEFT: Sluggerrr meets a young fan on top of the Royals' dugout.
ABOVE: This 1985 yearbook is highly prized among Kansas City fans.

TIMELINE

Steve
Busby

1969
The Royals play
their first season.

1973
Steve Busby pitches the
team's first **no-hitter**.

1971
Amos Otis is the
first Royal to win
a Gold Glove.

1977
The Royals win
102 games.

1984
Dan Quisenberry records
more than 40 **saves** for the
second year in a row.

Lou Piniella led
the 1969 team
with a .282
batting average.

Paul Splittorff
went 16–6 for
the 1977 Royals.

Bret Saberhagen and George Brett hug after Kansas City's 1985 title.

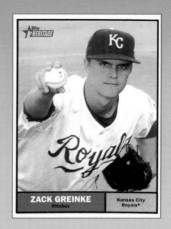

Zack Greinke

1985
The Royals win the World Series.

2003
Tony Pena is named Manager of the Year.

2009
Zack Greinke wins the Cy Young Award.

1990
George Brett becomes the first player to win a batting title in three different *decades*.

2011
Alex Gordon leads the team in home runs.

Alex Gordon

Q-RATING

During the 1980s, pitcher Dan Quisenberry and catcher Jamie Quirk both played for the Royals. They were the first "Q" pitcher-catcher combination in history.

HOT START

Zack Greinke won his first six starts of 2009, with an **earned run average (ERA)** under 0.50. Only two other pitchers in history had begun a season that well.

BO KNOWS EVERYTHING

When Bo Jackson got bored in batting practice, he would jump across home plate and hit left-handed. His teammates watched in awe as he smashed 400-foot home runs.

Big Names

From 1969 to 1975, the Royals had three managers who were later voted into the **Hall of Fame**—Joe Gordon, Bob Lemon, and Whitey Herzog.

Touching Them All

Willie Wilson hit 13 **inside-the-park home runs** in his career. No player since 1950 has hit more.

Arms Race

The Royals had seven hitters go to the All-Star Game before their first pitcher was chosen. Steve Busby finally broke the streak when he was named an All-Star in 1974.

Old School

In 1970, the Royals started a baseball academy. The team invited young athletes to learn the basics of good baseball. Frank White was the school's most famous "graduate."

LEFT: Zack Greinke   **ABOVE**: Bob Lemon

TALKING BASEBALL

"He was the greatest **clutch** hitter I've played with or against."

▶ *FRANK WHITE, ON GEORGE BRETT*

"I don't think I can play any other way but all-out. I enjoy the game so much because I'm putting so much into it."

▶ *GEORGE BRETT, ON ALWAYS GIVING HIS BEST EFFORT*

"I love it here. I love the fans. I love everything about this place."

▶ *ALEX GORDON, ON PLAYING FOR THE ROYALS*

ABOVE: George Brett   **RIGHT**: Bo Jackson

"It's all about the attitude, gut, heart, and determination to go out and give 120 percent every time to try and help the team win."

► **BO JACKSON**, ON WHAT MADE HIM PLAY SO HARD

"I'd rather be the shortest player in the **majors** than the tallest player in the minors."

► **FREDDIE PATEK**, WHO STOOD FIVE FEET, FIVE INCHES TALL

"The greatest personal satisfaction I've had is helping others."

► **EWING KAUFFMAN**, ON WHAT HE LIKED BEST ABOUT OWNING A BASEBALL TEAM

GREAT DEBATES

People who root for the Royals love to compare their favorite moments, teams, and players. Some debates have been going on for years! How would you settle these classic baseball arguments?

THE TRADE THE ROYALS MADE FOR AMOS OTIS WAS THE BEST IN THEIR HISTORY ...

... because they ended up with two All-Stars. Kansas City traded Joe Foy to the New York Mets for Otis and a pitcher named Bob Johnson. Otis became one of the best center fielders in the AL. Johnson struck out 206 batters in his only season with the Royals. The following year, they traded him for shortstop Freddie Patek. Patek was named an All-Star three times for Kansas City.

KANSAS CITY OF-DH
HAL McRAE ROYALS

THE TRADE THAT BROUGHT HAL MCRAE TO KANSAS CITY HAS TO BE THE WINNER ...

... because the Royals would have been lost without him. Kansas City got McRae (LEFT) from the Cincinnati Reds for two aging players. He showed his new teammates how to play the rough-and-tumble baseball that he had learned from stars such as Pete Rose and Johnny Bench in Cincinnati. McRae batted .293 after joining the Royals and had over 1,000 **runs batted in (RBIs)**.

WHITEY HERZOG WAS KANSAS CITY'S SMARTEST MANAGER ...

... because he knew how to build a winning team. Herzog (RIGHT) favored teams with good speed and defense. But he also knew the value of power hitters such as George Brett and John Mayberry. Throw in some tricky pitchers and a few smart guys on the bench, and you have what everyone called "Whitey Ball." What other manager had a *strategy* named after him?

WE WILL NEVER KNOW HOW GOOD DICK HOWSER WAS ...

... because he fell ill and died before he managed his sixth season with the Royals. Howser took over a club with a losing record in 1981 and led it to the playoffs three times in the next five seasons. In 1985, Howser guided the Royals to a great victory over the St. Louis Cardinals in the World Series. What was the best part of that championship? The manager in the St. Louis dugout was Whitey Herzog!

FOR THE RECORD

T he great Royals teams and players have left their marks on the record books. These are the "best of the best" …

George Brett

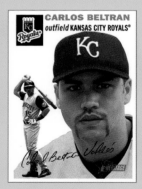
Carlos Beltran

ROYALS AWARD WINNERS

WINNER	AWARD	YEAR
Lou Piniella	Rookie of the Year	1969
George Brett	Most Valuable Player	1980
Bret Saberhagen	Cy Young Award	1985
Bret Saberhagen	World Series MVP	1985
Bret Saberhagen	Comeback Player of the Year	1987
Bo Jackson	All-Star Game MVP	1989
Bret Saberhagen	Cy Young Award	1989
David Cone	Cy Young Award	1994
Bob Hamelin	Rookie of the Year	1994
Carlos Beltran	Rookie of the Year	1999
Angel Berroa	Rookie of the Year	2003
Tony Pena	Manager of the Year	2003
Zack Greinke	Cy Young Award	2009

Bob Hamelin

ROYALS ACHIEVEMENTS

ACHIEVEMENT	YEAR
AL West Champions	1976
AL West Champions	1977
AL West Champions	1978
AL West Champions	1980
AL Pennant Winners	1980
AL West Second-Half Champions*	1981
AL West Champions	1984
AL West Champions	1985
AL Pennant Winners	1985
World Series Champions	1985

*The 1981 season was split into two halves because of a labor dispute.

OF

AL COWENS

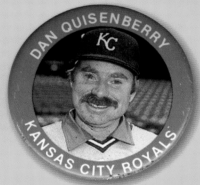

TOP: Al Cowens led the 1977 champs with 112 RBIs. **ABOVE**: Dan Quisenberry saved 37 games in 1985. **LEFT**: Whitey Herzog poses with pitchers Paul Splittorff, Dennis Leonard, and Doug Bird in 1976.

PINPOINTS

T he history of a baseball team is made up of many smaller stories. These stories take place all over the map—not just in the city a team calls "home." Match the pushpins on these maps to the **TEAM FACTS**, and you will begin to see the story of the Royals unfold!

1 Kansas City, Missouri—*The Royals have played here since 1969.*

2 Santa Monica, California—*Dan Quisenberry was born here.*

3 Chicago Heights, Illinois—*Bret Saberhagen was born here.*

4 Detroit, Michigan—*John Mayberry was born here.*

5 Glen Dale, West Virginia—*George Brett was born here.*

6 Brockton, Massachusetts—*Steve Balboni was born here.*

7 Brooklyn, New York—*David DeJesus was born here.*

8 St. Louis, Missouri—*The Royals played in the 1985 World Series here.*

9 Miami, Florida—*Dick Howser was born here.*

10 Toronto, Ontario, Canada—*The Royals won the 1985 pennant here.*

11 Monclova, Mexico—*Joakim Soria was born here.*

12 Manati, Puerto Rico—*Carlos Beltran was born here.*

David DeJesus

GLOSSARY

🧠 **AL WEST**—A group of American League teams that play in the western part of the country.

🧠 **ALL-STAR**—A player who is selected to play in baseball's annual All-Star Game.

🧠 **AMERICAN LEAGUE (AL)**—One of baseball's two major leagues; the AL began play in 1901.

🧠 **AMERICAN LEAGUE CHAMPIONSHIP SERIES (ALCS)**—The playoff series that has decided the American League pennant since 1969.

🧠 *ARTIFICIAL TURF*—A playing surface made from fake grass.

🧠 **CLUTCH**—Pressure situations.

🧠 *CONTENDER*—A team that competes for a championship.c

🧠 **CY YOUNG AWARD**—The award given each year to each league's best pitcher.

🧠 *DECADES*—Periods of 10 years; also specific periods, such as the 1950s.

🧠 **DRAFTED**—Selected during the annual meeting at which teams take turns choosing the best players in high school and college.

🧠 **EARNED RUN AVERAGE (ERA)**—A statistic that measures how many runs a pitcher gives up for every nine innings he pitches.

🧠 **GOLD GLOVES**—The awards given each year to baseball's best fielders.

🧠 **HALL OF FAME**—The museum in Cooperstown, New York, where baseball's greatest players are honored.

🧠 **INSIDE-THE-PARK HOME RUNS**—Home runs that do not clear the fence.

🧠 *LOGO*—A symbol or design that represents a company or team.

🧠 **MAJORS**—The top level of professional baseball.

🧠 **MINOR LEAGUES**—The many professional leagues that help develop players for the major leagues.

🧠 **MOST VALUABLE PLAYER (MVP)**—The award given each year to each league's top player; an MVP is also selected for the World Series and the All-Star Game.

🧠 **NATIONAL LEAGUE (NL)**—The older of the two major leagues; the NL began play in 1876.

🧠 **NEGRO LEAGUES**— Baseball leagues organized and run by Africans-Americans in the first half of the 20th century.

🧠 **NO-HITTER**—A game in which a team does not get a hit.

🧠 *PARALLEL*—Side-by-side.

🧠 **PENNANT**—A league championship. The term comes from the triangular flag awarded to each season's champion, beginning in the 1870s.

🧠 **PINE TAR**—A sticky substance used to give a hitter a better grip on his bat.

🧠 **PLAYOFFS**—The games played after the regular season to determine which teams will advance to the World Series.

🧠 **ROOKIE**—A player in his first season.

🧠 **ROOKIE OF THE YEAR**—The annual award given to each league's best first-year player.

🧠 **RUNS BATTED IN (RBIs)**—A statistic that counts the number of runners a batter drives home.

🧠 **SAVES**—A statistic that counts the number of times a relief pitcher finishes off a close victory for his team.

🧠 *STRATEGY*—A plan or method for succeeding.

🧠 **WORLD SERIES**—The world championship series played between the AL and NL pennant winners.

EXTRA INNINGS

TEAM SPIRIT introduces a great way to stay up to date with your team! Visit our **EXTRA INNINGS** link and get connected to the latest and greatest updates. **EXTRA INNINGS** serves as a young reader's ticket to an exclusive web page—with more stories, fun facts, team records, and photos of the Royals. Content is updated during and after each season. The **EXTRA INNINGS** feature also enables readers to send comments and letters to the author! Log onto:

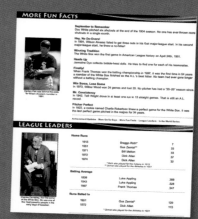

www.norwoodhousepress.com/library.aspx

and click on the tab: **TEAM SPIRIT** to access **EXTRA INNINGS**.

Read all the books in the series to learn more about professional sports. For a complete listing of the baseball, basketball, football, and hockey teams in the **TEAM SPIRIT** series, visit our website at:

www.norwoodhousepress.com/library.aspx

ON THE ROAD

KANSAS CITY ROYALS
1 Royal Way
Kansas City, Missouri 64129
(816) 921-8000
kansascity.royals.mlb.com

**NATIONAL BASEBALL
HALL OF FAME AND MUSEUM**
25 Main Street
Cooperstown, New York 13326
(888) 425-5633
www.baseballhalloffame.org

ON THE BOOKSHELF

To learn more about the sport of baseball, look for these books at your library or bookstore:

• Augustyn, Adam (editor). *The Britannica Guide to Baseball*. New York, NY: Rosen Publishing, 2011.

• Dreier, David. *Baseball: How It Works*. North Mankato, MN: Capstone Press, 2010.

• Stewart, Mark. *Ultimate 10: Baseball*. New York, NY: Gareth Stevens Publishing, 2009.

INDEX

ABOUT THE AUTHOR

MARK STEWART has written more than 50 books on baseball and over 150 sports books for kids. He grew up in New York City during the 1960s rooting for the Yankees and Mets, and was lucky enough to meet players from both teams. Mark comes from a family of writers. His grandfather was Sunday Editor of *The New York Times,* and his mother was Articles Editor of *Ladies' Home Journal* and *McCall's.* Mark has profiled hundreds of athletes over the past 25 years. He has also written several books about his native New York and New Jersey, his home today. Mark is a graduate of Duke University, with a degree in history. He lives and works in a home overlooking Sandy Hook, New Jersey. You can contact Mark through the Norwood House Press website.

ML   3/12